KING OF THE LUMBERJACKS

The Story of Joseph (Big Joe) Montferrand
and the Ottawa Valley Lumber Industry

Vincent J. Marquis

Published by Vincent J. Marquis

ISBN-13: 9780968505816
ISBN 10-0968505813

Cover design by: Art Painter
Library of Congress Control Number: 2018675309
Printed in the United States of America

AUTHOR'S INTRODUCTION

Imagine that you could travel back in time to the first half of the nineteenth century and encounter one of the most remarkable characters of Canadian History, a man renowned for his strength and courage. He did not fight in any war, but he toiled in a very dangerous occupation at a time when there was little law in the land beyond the big cities and towns.

His name has gone into folk legend under a corrupted form, and many improbable tales have been told about him, rivalling those of the American folk-hero, Paul Bunyan. You may have heard of him already as Joe Mufferaw.

You will have a guide on this adventure into the life and times of "Big Joe". Although the guide is a fictional character named François, someone like him could very well have existed and known "Big Joe Mufferaw". At any rate, the stories François has to tell are actually true, at least in substance if not in every detail.

François begins by setting the stage so you can better understand what happens. He needs to do this because we no longer have anything like the lumber industry as it existed between 1820 and 1860 in the Ottawa Valley and Western Quebec. This was the age of the "Big Timber". The description of the trees and the work François gives is real. The people he names in the stories are also real, and the events he describes actually occurred according to documented evidence given by eyewitnesses, although François' versions may be slightly different because of the personal perspective he has as Joseph Montferrand's good friend.

By remembering those "days of yore", we may appreciate our own times of ease and prosperity better and regain some sense of adventure. You will have to decide for yourself if you see Big Joe as François and hundreds of others who knew him did. To them, he was a hero and fighter who stood up for a downtrodden minority, and eventually began to win a measure of grudging respect both for him and the minority he personified.

François and I both hope you enjoy meeting the real Big Joe Mufferaw, Joseph Montferrand, a "Big Man" in more than the physical sense.

1. FRANÇOIS EXPLAINS

Bonjour! Je m'appelle François. I am French-Canadian and a lumber-jack. Of course, you must know what a lumber-jack is, *hein*? In the 1800s, a lumberjack cut down trees during the winter and in the spring moved them to where they could be sold.

Back in the old days, late each autumn, I would leave my farm near Montreal, and I would go with a group of young men into the 'up-country'. We travelled a long way, leaving Montreal in late October or the beginning of November, after the harvest was in, and we took a steam-boat up the Ottawa River. We might go up as far as Mattawa on the Ottawa, then take a trail, or build a road into the big timber. Once we arrived at our site, we would build a *chantier*, or lumber-camp, and we stayed all winter to cut the best big trees. Sometimes we followed another river that came into the Ottawa. We needed to be by a river or a lake connected to a river to bring the logs to the water in the spring. The water was our highway.

A lumber camp was not a very comfortable place. All the men slept in one big log cabin with many bunks around the walls. We had a big fireplace or maybe an iron stove to keep us warm, and not many windows. If there were windows, they were only small, and maybe not even made with glass, but with oil-paper.

There was often no chimney, but only a big hole in the roof ridge protected by a baffle to let out the smoke. Chimneys had a bad habit of catching fire, and then they might burn down our bunk-house and we would lose everything we had.

We always kept a big fire going. The English called the cabin a shanty, but this is just our French word *chantier* said wrong. And the men who worked there they called 'shanty men', but in French we are *bûcherons*, or *les hommes du chantier*. You see how we borrow words from the other language?

We worked very hard during the day. Our tools were not

complicated – axes of different sizes, both two-edged and one-edged, hatchets, mallets, mauls, sledge-hammers, ropes of different thickness and length, often run through pulleys, iron hooks and spikes and eyelets, gaffes, adzes, wedges, pry-irons and bars of iron. The work was very hard and could be dangerous.

In the shanty there were no private rooms. We did not have a bathtub or a shower. The toilette was a privy outside in the cold, with moss or old paper to clean ourselves. We had hard beds with straw mattresses, or even cedar boughs inside, and not a lot of blankets. We wore the same clothes all the time. We did not smell too good! We did not shave very often, so most men had big beards.

Up in the bush, I used to wear grey wool pants, a red or blue wool shirt of flannel, a coat made from a blanket that I tied around my middle with a red sash, boots of thick leather with big nails in the soles so I didn't slip, and a red, knitted wool *tuque* to keep my head warm. Some of us had mittens of rabbit fur, but many worked bare-handed because mittens got slippery. We would stop to warm up our hands from time to time by beating them or putting them in fur muffs or mittens. If you were swinging an axe with slippery mittens, your axe might fly out of your hands. Accidents were common and many men were badly hurt.

Most of us wore the same thing, but some had a different colour shirt or sash or *tuque*. Someone who saw me in a village or town would know right away, "There is a shanty man!"

We had lots of food, although it was always the same – fried salt pork, pea soup with salt pork chunks, fresh bread, boiled potatoes, sometimes refried in lard, oatmeal or pancakes with thick black molasses, turnips, and beans. We drank a lot of very strong tea with lots of sugar, and water. Coffee was too expensive. If we were lucky, we got apple pie and maybe a cake once or twice a week if the cook knew how to make it!

In the evening, we did not have much to do. So we sang and danced, told stories and jokes, and played the fiddle and the mouth organ or harmonica, and beat the time with spoons or sticks. Sometimes, someone might have brought along an accordion, and this was a great addition to our impromptu orchestra.

We played lots of cards. There was no alcohol allowed in the camp, and that was a good thing! If someone snuck it in, it would be taken and dumped on the ground. Alcohol makes men crazy when they are always cooped up, and some of them would get in fights and hurt each other.

It was different when we got to a town. Then some of the men who had money or could get credit in the taverns would become very stupid and use all their money to buy beer and rum and whiskey, and gamble, and go with different women. They would spend all their pay and have nothing to take home till they returned to the woods the next winter.

Other men had more sense, like me and my friend Big Joe. I went home to work on my farm and spend time with my family, to bring the cash money I had earned to help pay the bills and buy extra things we needed. Joe lived in Montreal, where he had some family to stay with, although he was not married in those days. He would also visit his many friends in other towns. If he did, he had to watch out for enemies too, although he was not afraid of anyone.

When we were in the camps, we had to learn to get along. Not everyone was always kind. Sometimes, we were with men from Scotland or Ireland, and there were Indians and Métis.

Some of the Scottish thought they were better than everyone else, and they would make it difficult for the others. Some of the bosses tried to keep the racial groups from being too mixed together in the camps, but this was not always possible.

If there were Scots, they considered themselves superior to the rest. They thought we French were better than the Métis, but maybe not as good as the Irish. But 'the frogs', which is who we French were to them, were at least better than the "half-breeds", which is the name they called the Métis, and the Métis were at least better than the Indians. That is what they thought. But fighting in the camp was not allowed, and you learned to accept the other guys not because of their skin or their language, but as men.

In the camp, there was no church. Maybe a few times a priest or a minister came to say mass or preach the Gospel. But most of the time, we didn't hear much about God, except maybe some men who swore and used His name to curse. Big Joe didn't like for his men to use bad language, but most of the time he just ignored it if it was not too serious.

Each day our jobs were to cut down trees, to clear the road, and to get the logs ready to move. The men were divided into 'crews' to do these jobs, with a 'crew-boss' in charge. We moved the wood to the river or lake-shore with sleighs and horses. We stacked them by the water-side to be ready for spring. In the spring, we put the logs in the water and we floated them out to the Ottawa to form into rafts.

We made different sizes of rafts, small ones for the small rivers and lakes. But when we got to the big river, we put the small ones together to make very large ones. We made them move and steered them with long oars and poles we made from the wood we cut. We made sails to put up too when the wind was favourable.

Some of the trees we cut to form into these rafts were 150-200 feet tall, and, maybe, six or nine feet across. Someone told me you have no more real trees today, except maybe a few in the far West or some forest the government did not let the shanty men cut down. You have machines to cut and move the logs you cut today. We had only the axe and later the long cross-cut-saw that takes two men to use, one on each end.

Here is how we cut the big trees. First, the axe-men cut a wedge to make the tree fall where we wanted. That was the 'front' side. Then they went around to the other side, the back side, to chop it through to the wedge. It might take 10 or 20 minutes to chop it right through. With a really big tree, two men swung their axes in the back cut, taking turns to make it go faster so that neither man would not get too tired. With the cross-cut saw they could go faster. When that monster of the forest began to move, everyone cleared out, running back and to the side in case the huge trunk jumped backward, as they sometimes did.

Sometimes, the tree might break while we were chopping or

sawing because the wood inside was rotten, but we couldn't see that from outside. That was also very dangerous, because if the tree broke, it could just go over sideways or backwards. So we always had a man watching to tell the choppers to run if that happened. Another danger was if the wind suddenly came against the tree and pushed it backwards or sideways from where the choppers or saw men wanted it to go. Again, the tree might go backwards or sideways. Even today with your machine-saws felling trees is dangerous work. For us, every year someone would be killed or injured in the camp.

Another way to get hurt was if your axe-handle broke, or the axe-head flew off, or your hands slipped when you were swinging, or you missed your cut and you let go of the handle. You might chop your own leg or foot or hit another man and hurt him.

I saw one man get killed when the head of another man's axe flew off and hit the other fellow in the back of the head! This was a terrible sight, with his brains leaking out through the crack in his skull! We had to bury in a pine coffin we built for him till the *curé* (priest) came later that winter to say the funeral mass for him. In the spring we dug him a better grave when the ground was not frozen.

Sometimes men got very sick and even died. An epidemic in a camp was rare, but a very bad thing if it happened. There was no doctor or nurse, and nowhere to go to get away.

Injured men who could not work could not leave the camp until someone could take them, if they were able to move. Sometimes one of the other men who was his friend would help him, or the foreman might make sure the hurt or sick men had someone to help them each day, to get them water and food, or to help them go to the privy.

To see a giant of the forest fall was a thrilling sight. The great tree began to fall slowly, then faster and faster, swinging down until it hit the ground with a great thump and crash that vibrated the earth all around. The axe-men then moved to the big body and trimmed all the branches off. Then they cut the huge trunk into logs, maybe 20 or 40 feet long. If it was close beside enough water, we might leave a big log, 60 feet long. These long logs were for the ships' masts of the British navy, or for the fast merchant-ships, the schooners. These logs of white or red pine were strong, long, and straight, so they were very good for masts. If we found oak, we kept it for the ships' planks.

We trimmed most of the logs to make them square. To do this, we chopped away the round arcs and knots. This allowed us to make the logs fit together in the raft, and they would also pack nicely into the ships when we get them to Quebec City. This wasted a lot of wood, but it was how the merchants wanted them, and we had to do this to sell them.

A big log could weigh quite a few tons, and to move it we kept special teams of really big horses. It would take a big team of horses to move a really big log. The men helped with long pry bars and gaffes.

When we got our logs to the waterside in the winter we piled them ready to roll down into the water. We waited for the ice to melt and the rivers to open in the spring. Then we unblocked the piles and the logs rolled down into the water. There we set them up in 'cribs', all lined up together in sections. The size of the cribs depended on the rivers and lakes we had to move them through to get to the big river, the Ottawa.

When we got the cribs to the big river, we built them into bigger rafts, and we took these down the river to Bytown, which is called Ottawa now. The town was named for Colonel John By, who built the Rideau Canal.

At Bytown there was the big Chute to take the rafts past Calumet and La Chaudière—the falls and big rapids that killed many a good man. Bringing a raft down through the chute was quite an exciting ride! In 1860, Prince Edward of England came and rode a raft through the Chute of *La Chaudière*. He was a brave man and loved the adventure.

We live on the raft as we moved it to Quebec City, our final destination. This trip could take six weeks, riding the raft and floating it along, getting it unstuck when it was stuck. When we had a problem, we used gaffes – long poles with hooks – or big curved spikes to grab and move and shift and lift the blocking logs.

The raft also had two or three row-boats lashed to its deck to rescue men who went overboard. We might also send a few men into a town we were passing to buy supplies we might be running short of.

In the rapids, we often hit rocks, and logs were pushed out of place. A big tangle could happen. The men had to jump and dance over the slippery logs like ballet dancers, and then used their poles and gaffes and spikes to undo the jumble. It was slippery and dangerous, and men could fall in between the logs and be crushed, or go underneath and drown.

As we lived on the rafts, we slept in little shelters or cabins. The cook made a fire on a sand pile or rock shelf to cook. If a fire 'got away' on him, of course there was plenty of water to put it out. The fire-bed rocks were covered with a thick layer of sand.

The water and wind were always moving us, so we could not stop even when we passed a town, as much as some men would want to visit the town to go to a tavern. If a man was so foolish as to go ashore, he would be left behind and lose his pay, after spending all winter and much of the spring doing all that work. If he managed to take a boat and catch up with the raft after leaving it, the Boss, in our case Big Joe, might very well tell him he was not welcome back.

Another reason we could not stop is that bringing the rafts downriver was a race to get our raft to the market-city as early as possible. Those who arrived first got the best price for their lumber! In those days of the really big timber, the market-city was Quebec, or maybe Montreal later in the season. Ottawa became a destination only after 1860 when much of the lumber was being turned into beams and planks for construction rather than for ship-building.

Finally, we would get our raft to Québec. There, the foremen like Bog Joe would haggle to sell the wood to the English merchants for the best price they could get. Each merchant's or company's rafts were joined into huge 'booms' waiting to be loaded into the many ships waiting to take this wood to England.

When this was all done, we got 'paid out'. Then we could go home till the next autumn. We could plant crops and farm, and be with our families. Some men just stayed in the town till they spent all their money, but that was really not wise or fair to their wives.

This way of life that I have told you about is all finished, gone with the big timber. The British stopped buying our wood after 1850 because it was cheaper to buy it from Sweden or Norway in Scandinavia in Europe. They began to build more metal ships in the later 1800s. Of course, people still needed wood, but it then went to the new saw-mills to make it into lumber – planks and beams for buildings and furniture. Even in your time, people still need lots of wood for building and making things. But much of your wood is made into paper, or chewed up and glued back together, not like the splendid logs and planks back in the time when Big Joe and I worked in the old forests.

These days, you no longer go up the big rivers by boat. In fact few people ever travel by river, except maybe to go fishing, paddle a canoe, or take a pleasure cruise. Your boats now go very fast, pushed by engines. But these are not steam engines. I would like to see this sight sometime!

I have also noticed that you rush around on smooth paved roads inside vehicles that move without a horse, pushed by the same kind of engine as the boat. You talk and listen to people far away over wires, like a telegraph with sound, or even without wires, and look at a box to see what people do all over the world.

You have other machines that fly at great speed through the air to take you to places far away. Your homes are full of many machines and gadgets that run on a power called electricity, and your life is very comfortable and easy. But I wonder if you are really happier than we were with our simple life back in the old days?

I hear all this, and I think, 'François, the world has become very fast and the people who have created all this are very intelligent. Maybe these people are living in the Millennium, *hein*?'

But I think the Millennium will bring peace, and everyone will treat everyone kindly and justly. From what I see, you do not have much peace, and many are not treated so justly, *hein*?

I often think about the beautiful big timber which I can find no more and which you will probably never see. How I would love to see one such tree now, not to cut it down, but to stand beneath it and look up, and think about where it comes from. Do you ever think about a tree like that?

Once upon a time, Canada *was* the big timber. When Jacques Cartier came with his little ship, what do you think he saw everywhere he looked? When the Natives moved so quietly through the woods, what do you think they saw? The big timber was their home.

The pioneers did not build their cabins with scrawny little trees. Their little houses had thick walls to keep out cold, and to protect the family from enemies and wild beasts.

Now you no longer live in a small dark cabin. You have a house with many glass windows, and electric lights – not oil lamps or candles. You have no kitchen fireplace, but heat with hot air blown around with motors through metal vents! You have a furnace in the basement. You have a basement! Amazing! You all live like kings! A person could think you must all be as wise as King Solomon himself!

Another thing that has greatly changed: many had very big families with 6, 8, 10, 12, 14 children! Sometimes it was very hard for us, I admit. But back then it was just how things were, how life was.

2. LES CANADIENS

Before I tell you about my good friend, *Le Grand Joe*, Big Joe Montferrand, I must explain about *les Canadiens*, as the French-Canadians called themselves back in those days. *Les Canadiens* spoke French, and they lived in Canada. To us it was not 'British North America', or an English country or colony. The English happened to rule, but Canada was our country long before they came.

You see, when the British defeated the French in 1760 during the Seven Years War, the French of France went home and left the *Canadiens* to look after ourselves. Even then, we did not think of ourselves as "Frenchmen", or even as "Frenchmen in North America". We already knew we were different from the French of France. We could not go back there anymore. It was not our home. Canada was now our home. Our ancestors had come and made a new life for themselves here.

At that time, in 1763, a famous, witty French fellow named Voltaire said, "Who cares anyhow? Canada is just a few acres of snow." The French government told the British, "You keep Canada, and we would like to get back those nice warm Caribbean islands, Martinique and Guadeloupe." The British had captured these islands during the same war when they conquered Canada. The British gave the back the islands and kept Canada, and some Englishmen said, "This not such a good deal, *hein!*"

We Canadians worried that the English would kick us out like they did to poor 10 000 Acadians in 1755. But the English realized that it would be very stupid and terrible to remove the 60 000 people of Canada somewhere else, and they said, "No, you can stay. You can continue to speak French and keep your religion and your civil laws. Just pay taxes and do what the Governor tells you, and we will leave you alone."

So we lived quietly for a while, and even supported the English when the Americans attacked Canada in 1775. But after about thirty years, some of our leaders realized that we needed someone to speak to the Governor so we would not always get a bad deal when the English merchants and bankers wanted new favours. The English hoped we would become English like them, so they let us vote, but they didn't listen to the Canadian members of the Assembly.

The British merchants had all the advantages and controlled much of the economy. For example, when Big Joe and I and many of our friends went up to the big timber each autumn, it was always the English who hired us, and the English merchants bought the wood and made all the big money. Even the Irish and Scottish, like the English, looked down on *les Canadiens*.

3. YOUNG JOE

Joe was born in 1802 in Montréal. His grandfather was a very big man. Great height and strength ran in the family. He had been a soldier in the French Army. When the French gave up New France to the English, the soldiers were given the choice to return to France or stay in Canada. Joseph Montferrand, the Grandfather of our 'Big Joe' chose to stay as he had married a Canadienne and had begun a family. A son whom they also named Joseph, the father of our 'Big Joe', had been born to them in 1754, even before the Seven Years' War began. All the Montferrand men were tall and very strong. The family was well known in Montreal for this characteristic.

Grandpapa Montferrand taught fencing and hand-combat techniques and was known as a very skilled instructor in what would have been the equivalent of your martial arts for those days. He wore a rapier, a fencing sword, much as the men of the 1800s in the United States wore a pistol, like a part of their every-day dress. He was renowned as the most skilled swordsman in Montreal.

His son, Joseph Montferrand II, joined the new North-West Company in 1783 and travelled far and wide in the wild country of the north-west to compete with the Hudson's Bay Company in the fur trade. The two companies were fierce rivals and when their crews met out in the lawless wilderness, they sometimes fought one another for the right to control the trade with the Natives in that area.

Papa Joseph did well and became an expedition leader with responsibility to guide, trade with the Native People, and bring the furs back to market. He was quite successful and was able to retire from this in Montreal and live very comfortably with his family. His reputation was one of courage, great strength, and skill in business. He was said to have never backed down in the face of intimidation or challenge, and to have never lost a fight either as a leader of his crew in the wilderness, or personally. He died in 1822.

Our Big Joe's Maman was born Marie-Louise Couvrette. Her ancestors were well-known in l'Assomption. Her mother was one of the famous Routhiers, a family well-known for their unusual height and strength as well. Marie-Louise was not afraid to challenge bullies herself when they were mistreating smaller people, not waiting for a man to be around to do so, and shaming men who were too afraid to step in.

Big Joe's father was also famous in the Montreal, as his father had been, and taught fencing and boxing, including a new form of it called *savate*, or kick-boxing. Boxing was a newly imported 'art', I will not call it a sport. The English brought it into the country.

Joe's parents were educated and sent Joe to school to learn to read, write, and handle basic mathematics. They wanted their children to practice their Catholic religion, respect God and live good lives, not spend their time idly and in ignorance.

Like almost all *Canadiens*, Joe went to mass on Sunday and took the sacraments. As a lad, our Joe was noticed for his consideration for other children, and his modest conduct. He did not use bad language, which was not tolerated in the Montferrand family.

He always believed in God throughout his life. He was taught to speak well and to be courteous, but told he must be able to defend himself. His father taught him well in this part of his education.

His brother was also a large man and was given the same instruction. Joe grew into a big man, very strong, like both his father and grandfather. He was very athletic and considered to be quite handsome. He enjoyed the company of young women but was always courteous and considerate with them. He would not back down from a challenge, although he did not go looking for trouble.

Joe knew he was strong, but was taught that this did not mean he should abuse others or take advantage of them because of his 'gift'. Rather, he had a responsibility to seek peace if possible and protect the victims of injustice and bullying.

In 1818, at the age of sixteen, had his first serious encounter with men of this sort. Three well-known "strong-arms" who were often hired by unscrupulous politicians to intimidate law-abiding citizens during elections came through Joe's neighbourhood. As they crossed over the lane on a footbridge, they stepped on the head of a child who happened to be underneath. They thought this a great joke.

Without thinking and in outrage, Joe leapt up from beneath and rapidly thrashed the three bullies with a mixture of rapid hand and foot manoeuvres. All the witnesses said they had never seen such artistry and coordination in a fighter. "It was more like a dance than a fight," said one witness. The three fled in humiliation with a warning never to return if they knew what was good for them.

His reputation spread rapidly, and soon he was often challenged by older, heavier men. He tried to avoid this business, but it did not stop, and if he refused a challenge, he was called a coward. His neighbourhood friends told him he had to defend his honour and that of their neighbourhood. His parents did not stop him, but warned him not to become conceited or a bully himself. At first they thought him too young for this rough business, but quickly accepted that their son was exceptionally strong and gifted even for a Montferrand.

In addition, substantial money could be won from the wagers in such contests. Within a year, Joe was considered the boxing champion of Montreal. In 1819 he went to Kingston to accept a challenge. In five rounds he beat a renowned professional hired by the British garrison to teach boxing.

Tragically, in 1822 both Joe's parents died of typhoid, one of those terrible fevers that were too common in those days before modern sanitation and cleanliness. Because of his grief, he left Montréal and went to work in the fur trade for the North-West Company, as his father had before him. He believed that a new adventure would help him overcome his great loss. He found Montreal too full of painful memories. He asked his brother to accompany him, but his brother decided to remain because he was courting a young woman.

Joe found that much had changed in the fur trade since his father's time. The two great competitors, the Hudson's Bay and North-West Companies, had both realized that there was no longer enough beaver and other furs for both to survive. The stock-holders directed the President to reach an agreement to join the two companies.

The North-West Company was bought by the Hudson Bay Company, and Joe quit and came back to Montréal. He did not care for the new bosses and what he saw as their unfair treatment of the *Canadiens*.

4. JOE BEGINS TO WORK IN THE BIG TIMBER

After two years of Joe being back in Montreal, a new lumber merchant named Mr. Bowman interviewed this big, strong man with experience of working in the wilderness and liked him. He was just beginning to explore the new opportunity of bringing big Canadian timber out of the vast forests north of Montreal.

The British wanted new sources for such timber for their navy and merchant ships because of the difficulties that had developed in their trade with the countries of northern Europe and the United States. Mr. Bowman was one of the first to begin bringing good replacement wood from inside the British Empire to make it accessible in the United Kingdom. Mr. Bowman hired Joe to take men up to work in the big timber. So, about 1827, Joe began to work in lumber.

That first winter working in the deep forests of the up-country was a hard one. There were as yet no towns or villages in that whole vast region. Bytown was still mostly a base camp for constructing the Rideau Canal.

Wrightville on the north side of the Ottawa River opposite Bytown was more developed, and the Wright family were the very first lumber pioneers who had actually shown that the big timber up the Ottawa River could be brought downriver to Montreal and then to Quebec City via the St. Lawrence. Steam boats were a new thing, and there were rapids to get around or go through, and this could be dangerous.

So when Joe brought his first crew up the river, they had to build everything from scratch. Of course, the men were mostly farmers who knew how to work hard and build cabins and sheds. We discovered that we needed more horses than we had brought, but the problem was that feeding horses where there are no farms means having to carry all their feed with us. We also had to build roads for them to work on in getting the wood to where we wanted it. This had to be done before we could begin harvesting the wood.

But then, we were cutting virgin forest, so for the first few years, we could simply take the best wood close to the shores of the river, or not far up one of the tributaries. Joe was also new at being a foreman, so the men had to learn to respect him, although his reputation helped a lot with that. With a lot of hard work and only a few injuries among us, we got our rafts to Quebec City in the early spring of 1828. Mr. Bowman met us there and was pleased with our work. He paid us generously.

In Québec that spring, a major of the British garrison at Québec heard that the *Canadien* boxing champion was in town. He wanted to prove that the British were superior to any *Canadien*. He insulted Canadiens as cowards and weaklings and challenged Joe to box in *la Place d'Armes*. Joe felt that he could not ignore this insult to his honour and his people, so he accepted.

Joe beat him real bad. He then returned to Montreal, but later that spring Joe was sent to accompany more rafts for Bowman and McGill (McGill was Bowman's partner) when they reached Montreal. He helped sell that wood to the English lumber merchants. In Quebec he stayed at *l'Hôtel de Québec*. The famous McConnell brothers had also brought rafts and held a big party for all the voyageurs and lumbermen at this hotel, the biggest in all Quebec.

Of course, the party was quite noisy and boisterous. There were complaints from some of the citizens of the city. The British soldiers in the garrison told the citizens to just stay out of the way and it would all die down. But the English navy officers decided to break up the party and sent sailors with clubs.

Joe was in his room at the hotel, because he was not a big drinking man. The McConnells came to his room and asked Joe to come down to help. They knew that the British had some respect for this big *Canadien*. So Joe came down and talked to the British officer and said, "Listen, monsieur. We have not come here looking for trouble. Why don't you let the men finish their celebration of finishing their work for this season? Then they will sleep it off and go home quietly and everyone will be happy."

But these English sailors didn't like Joe, because he had beaten their champion before, and so told him that they "don't take orders from a *Canadien* frog." Joe replied that he did not croak but crowed, so he crowed like a rooster and yelled, "*À tout faire!*" There was a terrific brawl, and Joe and the voyageurs and McConnells cleaned out the British. Many men had to see the doctors in the city. Every *Canadien* and lumberman in town came to see Joe and shake his hand for standing up for them.

5. JOE'S MOST FAMOUS BOXING MATCH

After this episode, the Captain of a British battleship in the harbour sent a message to Joe. "On our ship, we have the boxing champion of the whole British Navy. Let's see what a *Canadien* can do against him."

At first, Joe turned down this challenge, saying he was a peaceful man and no longer boxed professionally. The Captain suggested that he was afraid he would lose, and so lose his respect and reputation. Once more, Joe accepted because it had been made a question of honour.

This bout took place on the *Quai de la Reine* (Queen's Quay). Later, Joe told me that this was the only time he was ever afraid when he saw an opponent. The English champion was huge, very strong and all covered with hair.

Joe said to himself, "If I just go toe-to-toe with this man, he will beat me very badly." Joe decided to 'dance' and jab and tire out this big man. For 15 rounds, Joe wore him down. The crowd was not happy, and yelled, "Come on, Joe! Stand in and fight."

In the 16th round, he made a mistake, and got hit twice in the head. Joe backed away, and shook his head. He got very angry, and decided it was time to finish it. In the next round, Joe danced around him and till he found an opening. He put his two hands together and hit him twice like a sledgehammer in the ribs. The big man fell, and the fight was over. Joe needed two days in bed to begin to heal all his pains and bruises.

The Captain gave Joe $2000, but Joe told him, "I don't fight for money any more, but for honour or for a cause. You insulted me and my people. Keep your money and give it to that poor man I hurt. He needs it to get better. Just admit that I am the champion now."

"Well then," said the Captain, "Let me take you around the world and make you famous."

"No thank you," said Joe. "I could not stand to leave my country."

So Joe was a hero for French-Canadians in a time when everybody looked down on us. Over the years of working up in the timber camps and along the valley with its new towns and villages, people learned that it was not a good idea to insult us or assault us because of our language or religion. Joe would deal with those who did so if they would not apologize. He made lots of friends and enemies too. Every big man who thought he was tough wanted to fight 'the Big Frog', but no one ever beat him. Gradually, everyone came to respect him, even if only from fear.

But Joe did not hold grudges. He was willing to let bygones be bygones if the other fellow was also willing. If he occasionally lost his temper and started a fight, he apologized. He would stop before he hurt the other fellow too badly if his opponent said, "OK. I've had enough."

6. JOE AND THE SHINERS

One group that really hated Joe was the Irish at Bytown. These people had come there to work on building the Rideau Canal. They were promised farmland if they would stay on as settlers after the canal was built. Many of them did, and also worked in the lumber camps.

In Bytown, the Irish organised a gang called 'the Shiners'. Nobody really knows why they called themselves this. Maybe it is because they always gave you a black eye, *hein*?

The Catholic and Protestant Irish, called Orangemen, hated each other, but forgot their differences "to teach the frogs a lesson to stay in their proper place." They hated Big Joe so much they wanted to kill him, because Joe protected the *Canadiens*.

The Shiners in Bytown terrorized everyone, but especially the *Canadiens*. Even the 'respectable citizens' feared them, and the soldiers in the garrison on Barracks Hill (which is now your Parliament Hill) did very little to control them. In those days, Bytown had a very bad reputation as a lawless town.

The Shiners even burned down houses, beat men, tarred and feathered women, smashed up furniture, and committed many other crimes, but the magistrates never seemed able, or perhaps were not willing, to catch them. If they did, they and their families risked becoming targets themselves.

Now Joe would come to Bytown sometimes in the summer or fall to see people and recruit men for the winter-spring lumber season. In the mid-1830s, the Shiners decided to get rid of him. When Joe visited the Bytown area, he stayed in a house in Wrightville and crossed over to Bytown to visit his girlfriend by the footbridge near the great rapids of la Chaudière. One Saturday night Joe went to visit his girl as usual, and went home late.

The end of the bridge at Bytown was in the back-yard of an

inn. You had to go through the inn to use the bridge. The lady who ran that inn got money from the Shiners to tell them when Joe passed over to visit his girl. So she let them know that Joe had crossed over. The Shiner leaders told her, "When Mufferaw comes back, you lock the door at your end so he cannot go back." She did not ask any questions, but she knew very well that it was a trap to deal with Joe, their enemy.

Late that night, Joe came to the inn on his way home. He stopped for a minute and took a drink. When he went out the back door, Madame locked it, and Joe started over the bridge. When he got about half-way, he noticed something moving down at the other end and he stopped. Underneath his feet were the very dangerous boiling waters of the Chaudière. Many men had already drowned in this maelstrom before.

Joe looked hard to see what was at the end of the bridge; then the hair on the back of his neck stood up with the sense of danger he always had when his intuition told him a big fight was coming. So Joe yelled in his deep, loud voice, "Who is that over there? Come out and show yourself!"

Then he saw five, ten, maybe twenty men begin to move out onto the other end of the bridge, and a voice called back, "Hey, Mufferaw, we've come to take you home!" They laughed, "Yeah! We're going to take you home in a pine box tonight." At the back of this crowd two or three men were carrying torches. "C'mon, Big Joe," the voice said, "Don't you want to go home tonight?" and they all laughed again and began to walk towards him from the other side.

Now Joe is a brave man, but not a stupid one, so he decided the odds were a little bit high. He turned around and ran back to the inn. Of course, the door, which was never supposed to be locked, was locked. He pounded on it and yelled, "Lucy, open the door, quick!" But of course, she didn't open the door, and she did not even answer him. Then Joe understood. It was a trap!

Tell me, my friend, how would you react to this? What would you do? Joe was like a tiger when you put him in a corner, and he thought fastest and clearest when danger was worst. At this point, he knew that the Shiners had come not just for a fight, but to kill him if they could. He could jump over the side into the raging water, and he probably would drown because the water was very terrible in this place. Or, he could take his chance and fight. Joe thought, "Maybe I will die tonight, but no one will say that Joe Montferrand was a coward!"

He roared his battle cry at the crowd walking up the bridge, "*À tout faire!*" then crowed like a rooster, and ran full speed straight at them. The first six men in front went down like sticks when Joe hit them like a thunderbolt. Then, using *savate*, he began to hit every-which-way with his hands and feet, moving like a dancer with fists and feet of iron. He tossed four or five men over the side like sacs of grain into those terrible waters. The others backed off to regroup.

Then Joe saw a little man in front of him with a club. This gave him an idea. He growled at him, "You want to club me, my little rat?" He seized the hand with the club and crushed it, breaking all the bones in his wrist like little sticks. The man screamed, but Joe picked him up and said, "Now, you will be my club!" and he began to swing him like a club at the men in front who were hitting him and still trying to force him over the side. Bit by bit Joe smashed his way down through that gang, leaving bodies moaning behind, sending others over the side. Then, suddenly, the crowd broke apart before him and took to their heels, and those left standing in front turned and ran. Joe roared again with terrible fury and charged down after them. They had disappeared. He dropped his "club" there, and walked very fast to his rooming house. He felt terrible and spent days in bed full of bruises and very sore. I do not know if his 'club' ever fully recovered from the terrible pounding he received in the vice-grip of Joe's huge hands.

Witnesses who watched 'the battle on the bridge' from their windows afterwards said Joe beat 40 men that night on the bridge. One man drowned and two others died because of this fight, but Joe was clear because everyone knew he did not start it and he was only defending himself. Joe always felt very bad when he hurt someone really badly, and especially if someone died.

After this, the Shiners swore more than ever to get Big Joe and take revenge. They decided to put their boss, Martin Hennesy, against him. Hennesey was a very big, strong, tough man, even bigger than Joe. He bragged publicly that he would make Joe into mince-meat.

Joe took a job working in the woods near Buckingham, Quebec, and on his time off he went to that town to visit a friend who owned the hotel. When he went in he found 20 Shiners, with Hennesey, sitting in the dining room. Joe was wearing a brand new beaver hat that his boss, Mr. Bowman, had given him.

Hennesey said, "Hey, Joe, that's a mighty fine hat you got there."

"Yes," said Joe, "I'm glad you like it."

"You mind if I try it on, just to see how it looks on me?" said Hennesey. He walked over to Joe. Joe was a friendly fellow, always willing to let bygones be bygones and try to be a friend. Besides, he believed that it was best to let the other fellow start the fight, if that is what he was intending to do. So he decided to let Hennesey be the guilty one. Joe gave the hat to him and said, "Just have a mind that Mr. Bowman personally gave it to me."

So Hennesey got a wicked gleam in his eye, and said, "Well, now, this hat is too good for a d___ frog!" and he threw it on the floor and stomped on it, with all his gang laughing. Joe growled at him, with a red glare, "Just a minute, big man. You will have your brawl. But you will let my friend leave before this starts." He motioned to the owner to go out the back door and told him to lock it behind him.

Meanwhile, Mr. Hennesey's men locked the front door and made a circle around the two men. Joe was very angry and his deep voiced rumbled like distant thunder at the Irish gang-boss. "One way or another, you will pay me for that hat, Hennesey." Hennesey scoffed, "Come on then, you big frog!"

Joe crowed like a rooster, "*A tout faire! En garde!*"

The two big men had a terrible fight for many rounds until Joe finally smashed Hennesey like a rotten egg. Bruised and soaked in sweat, but still standing, Joe looked around at the others and said,

"Anyone else?" The other men just looked back, seeing their boss out cold on the floor. They got out of his way, although they had given him many kicks and punches from behind during the fight. That was the last trouble Joe had with the Shiners. After that, they left him alone whenever he came to Bytown, and *les Canadiens* in Bytown had less trouble.

7. JOE AND LA RIVIÈRE DES OUTAOUAIS (OTTAWA RIVER)

Another thing Joe was known for was saving people from drowning in the Chaudière Rapids. He was a very strong swimmer. In all, at different times, he pulled eleven people out of those terrible waters. One time, all by himself, he pulled a drifting boat to shore from the middle of the river. It took five big men to lift that boat out of the water.

I have two more stories of Joe on the River. One time, Joe was going up the river with a crew of 80 men to spend the winter in the woods cutting the big timber. They were on a little steamer called *Le Phoenix* with Captain Currie. These 80 men all got drunk, because in the camps the rule was no beer or rum to drink, so they drank a lot before they got there.

These drunk men began to make trouble for Captain Currie. As we have already said, Joe was not much of a drinking man, so he was sleeping up front in a cabin. Captain Currie was having so many problems with the drunk men that he finally went to Joe and woke him up. He said, "I am very sorry to bother you, Joe, but could you help me settle these men down to behave themselves, or they will wreck my boat and cause a shipwreck?"

Now Joe did not like to be disturbed in his sleep, so he got up without a word, put his boots on, and crossed the deck to the door of the men's cabin at the back of the ship. "Come out here at once, you bunch of pigs!" he yelled. The men were very angry at Joe, and they came charging to the door.

Of course, only one could come out the door at a time. Joe grabbed each one as he came, and threw him across the deck like a sack of potatoes into the corner against the wall of the front cabin and the rail, until there was an enormous pile of bodies. When he had finished, he growled at them all, "You will make no more trouble for Captain Currie, or it will be much worse for you. Now get to bed all of you!"

Captain Currie said he had no more trouble on that trip, or ever again when Joe was on his boat. He shook his head, and said, "It was the most incredible thing I ever saw. He moved with the speed of a cat, and with the strength of ten men!"

8. JOE'S "SIGNATURE" PAYS A DEBT

The other story happened one time when we were going up in the autumn to the work-camps. Now Joe as the boss knew the men had no money to pay for food because they needed to work in the winter to get money. So Joe paid supper each time they stopped at a hotel. But when the crew got to the last town before they were to go into the woods, Joe had no money left either. But he was too embarrassed to say so to the men or to Madame who kept the hotel. So Joe invited the men to eat and then said to Madame, "Madame, I am very embarrassed, but I have no money to pay you. I promise you when we come down the river in the spring, I will stop and pay you the bill." But Madame said to Joe, "*Non! Non!* Joe, it is my pleasure. You consider it a gift."

But Joe was unhappy, and he insisted, "Never! Joe Montferrand always pays his debts. You have to make a living. I promise you, I will pay the bill." But Madame was also a very stubborn lady, and she refused, "Non, Monsieur! This time it is my treat. You have been my friend many years. I will not take your money!" So Joe got very quiet for a few seconds, and then a big smile came on his handsome face, "Well then," he said with a twinkle in his eye, "If you will not take my money, I will pay you another way!" And he turned to the men at the bar and said, "You men stand back," and to the men at the table nearest to him, "And you men clear that table and those chairs back."

Now some of the men began to whistle and cheer, because they knew what Joe was going to do. They had heard that he had done this before just for fun, but they had never seen it done. And some of them had no clue because they had not heard that Joe was a master of *savate* and had the fastest feet and the highest kick in all of Canada. But the men who didn't know got very excited and asked, "Hay, Joe, what you gonna do?" or maybe asked a friend, "But what's he up to, hein?" And those that knew just said, "Ha!

Ha! You watch this. No one but Big Joe can do this!"

So with the way clear, and Madame standing back behind the bar, Joe took two steps backward, then bounced off one foot forward and landed on his two feet in a crouch. Then, without a pause, in one swift leap straight up from this crouch, he flipped his right foot straight over his head, pounded it on the planks of the ceiling, twisted as quick as a cat, and landed on his feet on the floor back in the crouch with his hands on his hips. The whole room exploded in cheers, whistles, stomps, and claps. But Joe whistled really loud and everyone quieted down.

Joe turned to Madame the inn-keeper, pointing at the ceiling. There everyone saw a black boot print, clear as anything, right where Joe planted his foot. "Now, Madame," says Joe, "You will not take my money, so I have left you my signature. So when your customers come in, you tell them to look for the signature of Big Joe Montferrand, and you show them. And then they will bring their friends to see, and you will get paid many times for many years because they will come to see where Joe signed your ceiling to pay his bill." And it was just like Joe said. People went to that place for many a year to see where Joe put his mark, and Madame made a lot more money that way than ever if Joe had paid his bill.

9. THE TRUTH ABOUT 'LE GRAND JOE'

There are so many stories about Joe. It is difficult to know which are true and which are not. I often hear many things said by people who never knew Joe. They say he was very mean and always looked for a fight to prove he was the toughest. I tell you that is a lie! Joe never ran from a fight, but he did not go looking for them. It is like anything when you have a reputation. Everyone who wants to prove something tried to fight Joe, until he beat everyone else, and then they left him alone.

Joe never met some of the other famous 'giants', but their friends say they beat up Big Joe, or that he ran like a coward from them. For example, some say Joe was thrashed by the McConnell brothers, but Joe and the McConnells were actually friends. They would meet in Montreal or maybe Québec and eat together, and talk about their *expériences*, their work, and even their fights. As I already explained, one time they even helped each other when the British police tried to arrest the crewmen of their two outfits.

Big Jim McConnell one time explained to me why he had no desire or need to fight Big Joe. Someone asked him why not, since he is bigger even than Joe. "Well, now," says this giant, "I can see you really do not understand about such things. Do you think we fight only for fun? I admit, I like to fight sometimes just to show a bully up. But Joe is not a bully. I respect Joe. He fights to protect himself, his men, and their rights.

"And if that is not enough reason for you why I do not fight Joe Montferrand, I will give you three good reasons from the side of the fighter", said Big Jim "1. I do not think I can beat him. You say, ""Why not?"" Because Joe only lost one fight in all his life.

"That was when he was a very young man back in Montréal. And that was not a fair fight. The other fellow attacked him from behind with a big stick on a dock, and Joe's foot got stuck between two boards so he could not turn around. Joe was beat unconscious, but when he got better, he went to look for this coward for three weeks, up and down the streets of Montreal. But no one would tell him where he was, because they knew Joe was too mad and might kill him when he found him. Finally, Joe saw him one day in the street and ran after him and caught him. The man was so afraid that he fell onto his knees and begged Joe not to hurt him.

"Most men would not hesitate to have revenge, but Joe is disgusted by a coward, so with one arm he lifted this man as big as him straight up so his feet were not touching the ground. Then Joe said to him, "Well then, you coward, I will let you go this one time. But I tell you this: If I ever hear that you have beaten anyone like you beat me, or that you have attacked someone smaller than you, or by treachery, like you did to me, be sure of one thing. Joe Montferrand will come after you and punish you twice—first, for what you did to me, and then for what you did to the other fellow! Now get out of my sight, and don't let me even see you in the same street as me again."

"So," Big Jim went on, "my first reason not to fight Joe is that he is no bully. In fact, he is an honourable gentleman—only a very tough one. A gentleman does not fight to prove anything, and Joe does not need to prove anything—to me, to the world, or to anyone else.

"The second reason I would not fight Big Joe is that he is my friend. I have met him many times, and he has always treated me with respect and courtesy. But I would never say he is afraid of me —he is afraid of no one, nor does he need to be. But the first time we met, we had both come to Québec with our rafts of big timber. That year Joe had beat me to market and brought in the first raft of the season and got the best price for Mr. McGill.

"We met in the hotel and we recognized each other at once by reputation. The men of our crews were watching very close to see what would happen, and, as you might guess, most of them expected us to 'go'. But Joe came right over to me with his famous, friendly smile and offered his hand to shake. So what does a man do when he sees there is no jealousy or desire to pick a fight, and no fear, but an offer of friendship? Well, I shook his hand, and he said, "Big Jim, I am Joe Montferrand, and I want to congratulate you on the fine way you bring down the timber and the way you manage your crew. I hear only good things about you. I was very lucky to beat you here with the first raft!"

"So how can you answer that?" said Big Jim. "With a punch in the nose? So Joe and I became friends. Sometimes we even helped each other out with our rafts if we met on the river, or helped the other guy to know how to best deal with such-and-such merchant.

"And so you say, 'But what is your third reason, Big Jim?' Well, I don't think I need a third reason. My first two are plenty good enough: Why would I fight a fine gentleman like Joe Mufferaw who is also my good friend? But since you insist on three reasons, my third one is this. Big Joe Mufferaw has the fastest hands and feet, and the smartest and coolest head that you will ever see in a fight.

"If the other man is bigger and maybe stronger straight on, Joe will dance and the other one cannot catch him to hit. Joe is a trained boxer, and a master of *savate*, the French art of fighting with the feet. He is not just a regular brawler. He knows how to wait, how to hit for best effect, when to hit. He can pick out the weak spot in the other man very quickly, and he will just keep picking at it until the other guy gets tired and weak. Then he moves in for the knockout.

"I said that Joe had the fastest hands you ever did see. I watched him fight only one time—against a huge Irish bully who beat up several of his men real bad. Our two crews had met up at Bytown on the way down the river that spring, and this Irishman had worked for another outfit from mine.

"I always told my men that if they started trouble with the crew of Big Joe, I would not wait for Big Joe to come—they would have to deal with me first. And Joe was very strict with his men —no fighting (except to defend themselves) when they were in his crew, or they were fired right away, and he would not protect them either if they started it. So Joe's crew never started trouble.

"Well, anyway, this big Irishman was a very big man, maybe three or four inches taller even than Joe. But Joe was much quicker and the Irishman could not get close to him. Joe would wait for the bigger man to let his guard down. Then Joe moved in like a flash, and his hands moved like a blur—three or four punches would get in before the huge man even knew what had hit him. Then Joe would dance back out, and bounce away before the giant could make even one punch. In all that fight, that man almost did not even touch Joe, but Joe knocked him cold, and he looked terrible when Joe finished with him.

"So, I am also a very big man—but I am not a stupid man. I would much rather have Big Joe for a friend than try to prove I am tougher than him and probably find out the same lesson as I saw him give to the Irish giant."

That, my friends, is the account of Jim McConnell, himself a legend of the Ottawa big timber. And so after a time, everyone left Joe alone, and they began to leave us Canadiens alone too, especially if we worked for or knew Joe. And that is one reason that Joe moved around so much—because he realized that he was like a protector, or an ambassador. And if bullies are never sure if they will have to deal with Big Joe for what they do, they often think twice, and on the second thought, they decide it is not so smart.

I have told you about how Joe became famous. Later, no one bothered him, and everyone respected him. He stopped going down the river with the rafts, or working in the camps in the winter. He worked directly for the big bosses, Mr. Bowman and Mr. McGill in Montreal, and he travelled to find timber and buy the rights to it, and plan the work to harvest a stand. He hired the men, and the bosses for the camps and the crews. He made good money, because he was the best in the business.

10. JOE'S SOFT SIDE

There is another side of Joe many did not know.

As I have said, Joe made good money for those days. But he did not spend it all on himself. He saved some, but he gave a lot away too. He always gave some to the church, but he had a big heart to help anyone who could not help himself.

For example, in 1837-8, there was the Patriot Rebellion in Lower Canada. I will not explain all of that very bad time, but just enough to help you know Joe a little better.

Because the English never listened to the petitions of the *Canadiens*, some *Canadien* leaders decided it would be better to throw the British out of Canada to start their own country, or maybe join the United States. Joe did not think so, and I agreed with him, so we did not join the revolt. In the winter of 1837-8 we went to work in the woods as usual, but when we came down in the spring of 1838, we heard about everything. Many of our friends, or their friends, their brothers, or their cousins fought. Some got killed, some wounded, and some went to prison.

All of this was very bad for the country, and very hard for the families. When we were paid out in Quebec City that spring, Joe went back to Montréal to help the people who had suffered. Everyone was afraid of being accused of treason, but Joe and help for these poor people and help them rebuild their lives. In my community, British troops had come and burned down the village church, taken my horse, and killed my cows and pigs for food for their army. They had given no money to pay anyone back, so I could not work the farm.

Joe came out to our parish to see what needed to be done. He told me, "Don't worry, François, I will see you get enough." And he did. He gave me enough to buy another horse, two pigs, some chickens, and a cow. He got my family food to last till the new crop came in. That is why I did not lose my little farm, and I am able to give it to my son now when I am an old man. Joe did many things like that for many people at that time, and at other times in his life, like during the Cholera epidemics.

Joe always believed in God. When he took his crews up and down the river, he always took them to church, and if le *curé* (the priest) or the minister came to camp, he would say to the men, "Alright, boys. The man of God is here, and we are all a bunch of sinners, so we are going to listen to him and we're going to church. And I don't want to hear you curse or swear while he is around."

Joe was not too worried about whether a man was a Catholic or a Protestant, because he said, "Well, I may be a Catholic, and that's all I want to be. But if a man is a good Protestant, I figure he's just as good as me. I think none of us knows for sure which is the true religion, but God looks at the heart. So I think that if we confess our sins, and keep a clean conscience, God will take us in when the time comes." So Joe helped many people on both sides, but he always stood up for his own people, *les Canadiens*, because everyone else was against us, *hein*?

11. JOE'S LAST YEARS

Joseph Montferrand when he retired and got married
(Bibliothèque et Archives Nationales du Québec)

Joe retired in about 1860. For the last ten years, Joe had worked as a boss all the time. Everyone respected him and everyone liked him, even his old enemies. He had no prejudices.

Joe finally got married after he retired. He always said he could not marry before because it would be unfair to any woman to have a man who was never at home to keep her company or help raise the children. But he was married only 2 ½ years before he died.

Joe was not like most people of that time. It didn't matter to him if you were *Canadien*, Scottish, English, Irish, Métis, American, Jew, or Indian. Joe only wanted to know what kind of man you were. Were you a man of honour, who told the truth, who did not cheat or bully the weak, insult or abuse a lady, or beat or abuse a child? Joe would always respect and help a good man. But Joe could not abide a bully, and he could never stand by if he saw the strong taking advantage of the weak.

What I have told you about the man many call Joe Mufferaw is true, as far as I know. There are many other legends about Big Joe, some of which may be true, or based on the truth. Many of them cannot be verified, so I have left them out of this account of his life.

The days of the big timber and the Bytown lumber barons are gone forever and can never return. Bytown became Ottawa in 1854, and by 1860, it was no longer the rough tough place it had been when Joe travelled the river. I think it is also safe to say, you will never meet another man like my friend, *le Grand Joe Montferrand*, or, as you call him, Big Joe "Mufferaw", King of the Lumberjacks and King of the Big Timber.

PHOTOS AND ILLUSTRATIONS

Hard at work squaring the big timber. (bytownmuseum.com)

You had to be careful, for it was easy to get injured, and sometimes men were killed.

A huge white pine in the Ottawa Valley
(bytownmuseum.com)

The timber slide at La Chaudière, Ottawa. The Prince of Wales went down this on a raft in 1860! It also shows the footbridge across to Wrightville. (en.wikipedia.org)

Timber ships loading up at Quebec around 1860. (en.wikipedia.org)

View of the Chaudière from 'Barrack Hill' (Parliament Hill) 1860, with the famous foot bridge where Joe fought the Shiners (MIKAN 2834130)

ACTIVITY SUGGESTIONS:

1.   Arrange a visit to a forestry museum and learn about the early lumber industry in your area.

2.   Take a tour of a lumber camp or a lumber mill to see how logs are transported to the mill and made into construction materials.

3.   Learn about the variety of trees and their uses in the Canadian forestry and lumber industries. Create a poster, collage, or report illustrating what you find out.

4.   Investigate how the pioneers cleared the land of timber and used the trees they removed.

5.   Research the stories of other "giants" of the early Canadian timber industry and do a report.

6.   Visit Ottawa and the Bytown Museum to find out more about the early days of Canada's capital city.

7.   Research the early history of Ottawa (Bytown) and the Ottawa Valley in the library and online. Present what you find out to a group. Make up a poster, or a slide presentation. Make sure you document your sources. (This project could be done with another student.)

SUGGESTIONS FOR FURTHER READING:

Finnigan, Joan. *Giants of Canada's Ottawa Valley.* Burnstown, Ontario: The General Store Publishing House, n.d. Photos, illustrations, maps.

Goyer, Gérard and Hamelin, Jean. "MONTFERRAND (Montferan), Joseph, dit Favre, better known as Joseph Montferrand." *Dictionary of Canadian Biography, Volume IX, 1861-70.* University of Toronto/Université Laval, 1976-2020.

Guillet, Edwin C. *Pioneer Days in Upper Canada.* Toronto: University of Toronto Press, 1963. 216 pp. Photos, maps, illustrations.

Legget, Robert. *Ottawa Waterway, Gateway to a Continent.* Toronto:University of Toronto Press, 1975. Maps, illustrations, photos, index.

Mika, Nick & Helma. *Bytown, the Early Days of Ottawa.* Belleville, Ontario: Mika Publishing Company, 1982. 257 pp. Illustrations, maps, index.

Newton, Michael. *Lower Town Ottawa, vols. 1 & 2.* Ottawa: National Capital Commission, 1981. Manuscript report 106pp.. Maps, photos, index, diagrams. A wealth of information about the details of part of early Ottawa from 1827 to 1900.

Sulte, Benjamin. *Histoire de Jos. Montferrand, l'athlète canadien.* Montréal: Imprimé et publié par Camiré et Braseau, 1884. Public domain in Canada. e-book facsimile on Project Gutenberg Canada, Oct. 18, 2008

Taylor, John H. *Ottawa, an Illustrated History. The History of Canadian Cities.* Toronto: Canadian Museum of Civilization,

1986. 232 pp. Maps, illustrations, photos, index, tables.

Walker, Harry & Olive. *Carleton Saga*. Ottawa: Harry J. Walker, 1968. 571 pp. The definitive study of the history of Carleton County, the area of Ontario surrounding Ottawa. Maps, illustrations, photos, index.

Woods, Shirley E., Jr. *Ottawa, the Capital of Canada*. Toronto: Doubleday Canada Ltd., 1980. 350 pp., photos, maps, illustrations index. The definitive general history of Ottawa.

Photo credits:
All photos are public domain and taken from a variety of internet sources, as indicated within.

ABOUT THE AUTHOR

Vincent J. Marquis

Vincent is a retired educator with almost forty years experience. He has loved history since childhood. He is a husband, father, and grandfather. Over the years he has given seminars and workshops on a variety of topics, largely historical, from coast to coast in Canada. He is a gifted communicator at relating history as the story experienced by the people involved. He has imaginatively retold episodes from Canadian History and written an easy-to-read biography of a Father of Canadian Confederation. He continues to work on a number of new projects.

BOOKS BY THIS AUTHOR

King Of The Lumberjacks

The true story of the legendary Big Joe Mufferaw, and the Ottawa Valley Lumber Industry from 1830-60.

The Last Stand Of Dollard Des Ormeaux

The tale of an epic battle in 1660 in early Canadian History. A small band of French volunteers and some of their aboriginal allies meet a large Iroquois force planning to destroy the French settlement of Ville Marie (Montreal). The story is told from the standpoint of Pierre Radisson, a famous Voyageur who came upon the battlefield some days after it ended, and heard the details from eyewitnesses.

A Truly Loyal Subject

An easy to read biography of George Brown, one of the key Fathers of Canadian Confederation. Brown was the kingpin or catalyst in starting the process in 1864 that ended in Canada's creation as a true nation in 1867. He was also Sir John A. Macdonald's long-time main opponent, but sacrificed his career to bring about Canada's national unification.

Grandpa's Hands

The story of the unexpected friendship of a grandson with his curmudgeonly grandfather, a hardened veteran of the Great War.

Grandpa opens himself to his persistent grandson and shares his true story of war and its effects. It changes them both. The author is the grandson in this true story.